The Women's Simple Guide to Investing

Elinor Davison

**"Give a man a fish, and you feed him for a day.
Teach a man to fish, and you feed him for a lifetime."**
"Anonymous"

Author: Elinor Davison
Illustrator: Barak Davison

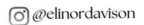 @elinordavison

Contents

Introduction

Welcome to The Women's Simple Guide to Investing. When I started investing in the stock market I have noticed that most of my girl friends had no idea about investing in stocks. They actually had no clue about investments in general. It is not because they are not clever. The opposite, they are all very knowledgeable, capable and have great jobs. But no one ever taught them about investments; or expected them to know anything about it. I found that many women live their lives without having a clue about how to make money other than from their day job. This is how the idea of this book came up.

I tried to explain the terms in the shortest and easiest way I could. I have used simple language with no big words that nobody understands. You can either read it in order or just open random pages and flick through it.

I hope that when you finish reading this book you will understand better the basics of investments and you will start planning your financial future and begin investing yourself.

If you want to improve your financial situation, first of all, you need gain some financial knowledge.

Well, it doesn't mean that you should start reading the Wall Street Journal on a daily basis but just start learing the basic terms. You will suddenly notice that investments are all around you. Next time you hear people discussing investments you will slowly start to understand and pick it up, just like a new language.

Knowledge is power and expanding your financial knowledge will give you the power to take control and plan your financial future .

You will be surprised that investments and financial terms are not as complicated as they may first seem.

Let's start...

'If you believe in yourself,
anything is possible'

Chapter 1

Why do we need
to invest our money?

First of all, let's understand why people make financial investments.

You probably ask yourself:
Can I not just earn money from my day job, save some money in a savings account in the bank with minimal interest and be worriless?
The answer is: of course you can.

But... what will happen if you can't work for a while, or if you want to take a break from work, maybe to raise a child and stay at home, maybe go on a trip around the world, maybe start your own business, and of course when you get older and would like to retire.
Even though we just want to live in the moment and enjoy life, we had better plan now for our unknown future. Yes, I know it's not fun but **I don't know anyone who saved and invested and regretted it later on. But I definitely know the opposite ...**

Why do people invest their money?

People invest their money for three main reasons:

1. They want to create a passive income.
2. They want to keep the value of their money.
3. They want to grow their wealth.

Why should we not keep our savings in an account at the bank that produces minimal interest?

Simply, when our money sits in the bank and is not invested it loses its value every year.

What does it mean that our money loses its value, and how does it happen?

Let's use an example:

Today you have $100 in the bank.
You can buy with that money a shirt in your favourite store.
Three years from today, you will no longer be able to buy that specific shirt! Because in three years it will cost more than it cost today. Production, salaries, rent, all go up and that's why the price of the shirt will also go up.

As a fact, if you keep cash in the bank for few years untouched, you won't be able to buy the same things you can buy today with that same amount of money.

Over the years goods and services become more expensive. Therefore, you "lose" money when your cash is not invested.
This is caused by inflation.

What is Inflation?

Inflation is the ongoing rise in the cost of living. Every year the prices of the food we eat becomes more expensive, the haircut we have, the manicure we often do, the dry cleaning services we use, etc., all become more expensive every year. Even if we don't always notice it. It happens!

_____

Why do you need to care about inflation and how does it impact you?

I guess you don't want your hard earned, saved money to lose its value. The understanding that money loses its value throughout the years is the main reason you should invest your money. You should aim that your money will be invested at least in a way that will keep up with inflation.

Chapter 2

Passive Income

What is passive income?

A big part of the idea of
investments is passive income.

Passive income is money
earned with minimal work, effort,
and time. Sounds amazing
doesn't it?

How can you create a passive income?

There are quite a few ways which you can create yourself a nice passive income.

You can invest your money in the most common investments which are:

- **Property**: such as buy to let.

- **Stock market**: with shares and bonds.

- **Alternative investments** such as cryptocurrencies, NFT's (non-fungible token), gold, etc. (alternative investments are riskier and not suitable for beginners and so, I will not go further).

There are many ways other than investments that can produce a passive income. Renting your home when you are away is one example or renting out your car is another idea. Creating a successful video on YouTube can also produce a passive income.

With a quick internet search you can find an idea that is suitable for your skills and lifestyle. In this book we focus on financial investments.

What's so great about passive income?

Passive income is like having a second job but without putting the extra hours and effort to it.
When you create yourself a passive income you earn extra money when you are on holiday, when you are asleep, when you are unemployed, and when you are retired.

Passive income is great!
It will give you peace of mind and freedom in the future.

So, you love the idea of passive income and you want to start investing but you don't have any extra money.

How can you start saving?

Start by saving what you can:
-it can be making lunch at home,
- or dropping one cup of bought coffee a day,
-or sticking to a shopping list.

You can start by saving $20 a week.
Over five years' period that can
turn out to be $5200.
($20x52 weeks=$1040 a year's
$1040x5 years=$5200).

You don't have to be rich to start investing.
You can start by investing $50
a month. That's much less than
one cup of coffee a
day.

Chapter 3

Financial terms, calculations, yield, and return.

When people talk about investments they talk in terms of yield and return.

It may sound really complicated but it really isn't. The reason you need to understand those terms is to have a better understanding of the investment you are going to make when you will make one.

What is yield?

Yield is the income we get from an investment.
It is calculated as a percentage (%).
We get yield from investments such as:

-shares
-bonds
-properties to rent

What is return?

A return is how much money
we have earned or lost
from an investment.
We can make a positive return, when we
earn money.
We can make a negative return, when we
lose money.

———————————

What's the difference between Yield and return?

-Yield is the percentage % we get each year.
-Return is the actual amount of
money we've made (or lost).

Generally speaking:
Yield is looking forward when
planning the investment.
Return is looking backwards,
it's how much money we have
earned (or lost) from our investment.

How do we calculate yield%?

$$\frac{\text{Yearly profit from our investment}}{\text{The total amount we've invested}} \times 100 = \text{yield \%}$$

For example
We invested $10,000 in shares.
At the end of year our profit was $800.

How do we calculate our yield?

800(yearly profit)/10,000(investment)=0.08
0.08x100=8%.
We have made 8%
yearly yield on the $10,000 investment

$$\frac{800}{10,000} = 0.08 \times 100 = 8\%$$

-Note that we calculate yearly
yield not monthly!!

Calculating gross yield* from a buy to let property:

I paid $200,000 for my property. The monthly rent I earn is $1,000. My yearly rent is $12,000 ($1000x12 months).

$$\frac{\text{Yearly rent}}{\text{property price}} = \text{gross yield.}$$

Therefore, my gross yield is
12,000/200,000=0.06
0.06x100=6% yield.

$$\frac{12,000}{200,000} = 0.06 \times 100 = 6\%$$

*Gross yield is yield before expenses are deducted.

Chapter 4

Stock Market investments

When you buy stocks and shares, you have no responsibilities towards the company issuing them. You will not have the big expenses that may incur when you invest in a property.

On the other hand, **share prices go up and down** and you must never forget that **share prices don't always go up**.

The good news, however, is that **over the years, the stock market generally goes up**. Even if at times it falls, in most cases it will continue to rise at some stage later.

Is Investing in the stock market like gambling in the Casino?

No, it's not.

When you invest in the stock market you can conduct a research. When you play in the casino it's purely luck.

Many stock markets exist across the world, but most important ones are **New York, Tokyo and London.**

_____

Main USA stock market indexes:

- S&P 500 .
- Dow Jones Industrial Average (30 largest companies).
- Nasdaq (National Association of Securities Dealers Automated Quotation).

_____

Main UK stock market indexes:

- London FTSE 100 (The Financial Times Stock Exchange pronounced as footsie).
  It is a list of the 100 largest companies listed on the London Stock Exchange.
- London FTSE 250 (the next 250 by size).

What are shares?

Here is a short and easy
explanation of what shares are.

For example, this bag is a company.
It's divided into many little squares,
which are the company's shares.
When you buy shares, you buy
little squares of the company, so
you become a small part owner of
the bag (proportionate to how
many squares you have purchased).
When you buy the shares of a
company you become a small part
owner of the company. You
become a shareholder.

Why do companies trade on the stock market?

One short answer is to raise money.

When a company wants to raise money, it can start trading on the stock market.
A way for the company to raise money is to sell shares to investors. The investors then become shareholders.

It means they hold a share/.i.e a piece of the company.

What makes share price go up and down?

It is very simple, it's all about supply and demand.
If more people want to buy a share rather than sell it, the share price will go up because the share is more 'in demand' and vice versa.

———————————————

Nowadays it's very easy to invest in the stock market. There are many apps that allow you to invest directly into stocks and shares.

———————————————

Tip: You can start investing in the stock market by investing in a company that you know and that you use yourself and believe in.

What is a dividend:

A dividend is when a company shares its profit with shareholders (can be you if you own shares).

_____

When a company earns a profit, it is able to pay a proportion of the profit as a dividend to its shareholders. Therefore, when buying shares, it's important to check if the company gives shareholders dividends. Some companies pay dividends quarterly, every six months or yearly (or not at all).

_____

If you bought shares that pay dividends to shareholders you should get some back as a return for your money. It is proportionate to how much you have invested.

Facts you need to know:

You should get dividends
regardless if the
share price goes up,
or goes down.

* Also note that companies
sometimes cancel dividend
payments.

_____

Note:
Not all companies
give dividends.
You should check
before purchasing
the shares.

You can gain money from shares in two forms:

1. **Dividends**.
2. **Capital gain**- when the share price goes up.

When you invest in shares you should do your research and buy shares of companies you believe in and you think will continue to grow.

**Make the economy work for you
rather then you only working for
the economy.**

For example:

I love shopping at Gap so I bought
shares in Gap.
I believe in the brand, and I shop
there. I might as well benefit from
it.

I fly with British Airways I,
therefore, bought shares in British
Airways.
And so on...

It's funny but the stock market is a
lot about psychology.

When people are happy they
have the confidence to buy shares,
so share prices go up in value .

When people are scared or
worried
they sell their shares and share
prices go down in value .

Risks:

Naturally when you make
an investment of any
kind you are taking a risk.

You can choose to avoid
taking risks.

But you should take into
consideration
that you also avoid taking
the chance to succeed.

Let's learn some stock market talk:

Bullish v Bearish

-Are you 'Bullish'?
An investor who believes share
prices will go up.

-or are you 'Bearish'?
An investor who believes share
prices will go down.

Bull market:
Share Prices
Go up.

Bear market:
Share Prices
Go down.

What can make a company share's price to go up?

- The company has a big new product coming up.
- Prices and demand for what the company does are growing fast.
- The company is expected to make profits, that beat predictions and forecasts.
- The company looks like it's undervalued in comparison to its rivals.
- A takeover bid is on the cards.

What is Market cap (market capitalisation)?

It means the value of the company.

How is it determined?
Share price ✖ the number of shares= market cap

———————————

Do you know that around 85% of the value of the stock market is owned by big investors such as pension funds, insurance companies and trusts?

What is an IPO?

Initial Public Offering:

- The process of bringing a company into the stock market is known as an IPO.
- You can buy shares through an IPO.
- It is more of a risk.
- If you have faith in the company hold the shares as long as you can.

Don't forget you may have to pay taxes on your share gains.

Part of the investment process involves taking some risks.

If you would like to minimise your risks, you can invest your money in safer investments. These may give you lower returns but are considered less volatile and allow you to sleep better at night.

Once you have decided you want to start investing your money, **you need to determine what return you want from your investment**.

- Do you want to keep up with inflation?
- Please note that the present inflation rate is extremely high. We refer to normal times (typically 2.5% annual growth).
- Do you want to have a moderate Return (4-5%)?
- Or do you want higher returns which normally comes at higher risks (6% and up)?

Chapter 5

Bonds

What are Bonds?

- To make it simple, a bond is when you buy part of a debt.
- A bond is a loan made to a company or government that can be traded on the stock market.
- When a company needs to raise money but doesn't want to sell shares in return, it can issue a bond.
- Bonds are usually fixed interest investments.
- Bonds are for fixed terms.
- That means that you should be able to calculate before the loan starts how much money you will make by the end of it.
- Bonds usually count as lower risk investments.
- Bonds are often referred to as 'one step up from cash in the bank'.
- Bond interest is usually paid twice a year.
- You can buy or sell bonds part-way through their lives. You may get more or less than what you paid.

An example for bonds :

A government needs money to invest in education and roads.

They issue a new bond to raise $100,000,000.

-You buy $10,000 of that.
-The interest promised for that loan is 5% ($500 a year).
-You receive $250 twice a year.
-The bond is for 5 years which means that at the end of the 5 years you will receive your initial investment of $10,000 back .
- You know before the loan has started, that at the end of the five years' term you would have made $2500 interest ($500x5) and you have kept the initial amount you have invested which is the $10,000.

*This is assuming the government doesn't go bust... (countries have credit ratings and the better the credit the safer the bond).

The pros of investing in bonds:

- You usually invest your money for a limited amount of time.
- You receive interest for the money you have invested on a regular basis.
- When the loan expires you receive the initial face investment value back.
- You didn't spend this money, and you enjoyed the interest you received over the years when it was locked in the bond.

Why should you consider investing in bonds?

- If you are a cautious investor.
- If you need the money for something specific in the future such as education or a special event, you know that after the loan period ends you will receive the face value of the bond back, i.e the whole amount of money that you have invested.
- If you are retired and need certainty of income from your savings.

What are the differences between shares and bonds?

- Bonds raise money via debt.
- Shares raise money via giving investors a stake in the company.
- Shares are permanent. They can go on forever unless a company ceases to exist.
- Bonds are usually for a limited amount of time.
- Shares pay dividends.
- Bonds pay interest.
- Shares give you legal rights in the company.
- Bonds don't.

Things you should know:

Share prices can go up and down and as a shareholder you may worry how well the company is doing as it affects the share price and the dividend's payment.

Bond holders need to worry less, as bond interest is not affected by performance and **if the company ever goes bust, bond holders can be the first in line to get their money back.**

Chapter 6

Property Investments

Property is a popular investment. It is tangible and it gives people a sense of security when they own a house or an apartment.

It is, however, an expensive investment, and you need a substantial sum of money to buy a property.

———————————

Why do people like property investments so much?

Because property is a solid investment. Property rarely loses its value over longer periods.
A property investment can not just go up in value, it also produces an ongoing rental income.

The three most popular ways to invest in property are:

1. Buying your own home (some would claim it's a liability rather than an investment).
2. Purchasing a 'buy to rent' property.
3. Buying shares in property companies.

Why did I mention that buying your own home is not an investment but a liability?

Because when you buy a home you need to spend money on your mortgage, fixing the house, paying insurance etc.

It is not an investment that pays you money but the opposite, it makes you spend.
If something you bought pays money into your account, it's an investment.
If it makes you spend, it's a liability.

On the other hand, instead of paying rent you will be paying your monthly mortgage, and over the years the price of your home will probably go up in value, so instead of spending the down payment you have kept the value of your money.
You should, therefore, do the calculation before purchasing a house and make sure it is the right financial decision for you.

When buying a property, you should take into consideration the following extra costs:

- Taxes.
- Real estate agent's fee (in some countries the seller pays, some the buyer and some both seller and buyer).
- Legal fees - lawyer, title registration etc.
- Surveyor- you may need a surveyor to secure your mortgage.
- Any adjustments/improvements you wish to make to the property once it's bought.

You don't need the whole amount of the property's purchase price in order to buy it. You can purchase a property with a mortgage and merely pay a down payment (it can be as little as 10% of the purchase price).

———————————

What is a mortgage?

A mortgage is a loan you take from a bank or a building society to purchase a house/apartment/shop.

It is paid monthly over a long period of time – typically for 25 years.

There are two main types of mortgages:

1.Interest only mortgage- where you just pay the interest on your loan every month.
At the end of the mortgage term you will need to pay back the full amount you have borrowed so you can own the property. If you borrowed $150k you will need to pay it back in full.

2.Conventional mortgage- you repay monthly, the amount you have borrowed plus interest. While the monthly payments are higher than an interest only mortgage, when the mortgage term ends you own the property. If you borrowed $150k you have already paid it and the interest over the years. You don't owe anything at the end of the mortgage term. The property will be fully yours.

What should you consider when taking a mortgage?

- You should calculate how much money you can afford for the down payment.
- You should also calculate what monthly mortgage payments you will be able to pay comfortably.
A tip:
- Once you have figured out what your monthly mortgage would be, I suggest you calculate the total amount that you will pay for the property by the end of the mortgage term (add the interest you will pay over the years).
That's how you will know the total sum you will pay for your property.

————————————————

You may ask yourself:

I have all the cash, should I buy my home with a mortgage or should I put all the money into my home?

Financial advisors will generally suggest you to take a mortgage if possible and invest the money you have left as an investment that will produce a passive income.

You should know that **when you purchase a property either to let or live in, it comes with responsibilities.** When something goes wrong you must fix it straight away as it may damage your neighbour's property or cause more damage to your property in the future.

Moreover, if the property happens to be empty you still have to pay the bills. Some properties have management fees and other expenses. You should be aware of that and take into consideration other unpredictable costs.

Of course ,when you have good tenants and you receive a monthly rent, property can be a great investment!

What is a property's net yield?

Net yield is what you gained
after you deducted the expenses
you spent on the property
throughout the year.

It is the true yield you are left with
at the end of the year.

How do we calculate the net yield for a rental property?

We calculate the property's yearly
rental income
Minus-
expenses such as estate agents' fee,
service charges, repairs, mortgage
payments, etc.
we divide that sum by/
the property purchase price including
expenses such as
lawyer, estate agent's fee, taxes
x100= net rental yield %

For example:

How do we calculate the net yield for a rental property?

Our property's yearly rental income is $20,000.
We deduct from that sum our expenses such as estate agent's fee, service charge, repairs, mortgage payment, etc.
Our total expenses came up to $6,000.
We are left with **$14,000 net income** after we deducted our expenses (20k-6k).
We then calculate the property's total purchase price. We bought it for $200,000.
Our expenses on top were $20,000 (lawyer, estate agent, taxes) we paid for the property a total sum of **$220,000**.
We divide the net income by the total purchase price.

14,000/220,000=0.06x100=6% net yield for our rental property.

$$\frac{14,000}{220,000} = 0.06 \times 100 = 6\%$$

You may hear the term ROI when looking at a property investment.

What does ROI stand for?

Return on Investment.

How do we calculate ROI?

Out Net Profit (profit after we deducted our expenses) / Actual cost of the investment x 100= ROI%

We don't calculate ROI from the price of the property but from the amount we have invested.

In that case **if we took a mortgage, we would calculate the down payment plus all the expenses. Not the whole property purchase price.**

For example:

I bought a $100,000 property.
My down payment was $20,000.
I had a 10% extra costs of $10,000 on top
of the down payment.

The total amount I invested was **$30,000**.

At the end of the year, I gained a net profit
of **$3,600** from my rent.

To calculate my ROI, I divide my net profit
of $3,600 by the $30,000 I invested
=0.12x100=12%
My ROI is 12%.

$$\frac{3600}{30000} = 0.12 \times 100 = 12\%$$

Net Yield:
**In comparison, the net yield without a
mortgage would be my net rent divided
by the property price.**
 3,600/110,000=0.032x100=3.2%
(rent)/(property price)

$$\frac{3600}{110000} = 0.032 \times 100 = 3.2\%$$

When selling a property
Don't forget to calculate your
selling expenses, such as:

- Repaying your mortgage.
- Estate agent's fees.
- taxes.
- legal fees.

Always calculate your expenses
in advance to avoid any
surprises after the sale.

Chapter 7

Interest and credit score

What is an interest rate and APR?

An interest rate is the amount a lender (a bank for example) charges the borrower. **It is the cost of the loan.**
It is calculated as a percentage % of the amount loaned.
The interest rate on a loan is calculated on a yearly basis, known as the annual percentage rate - APR.

The lower the APR the better it is for you.

Why is the current interest rate important to you?

- When interest rates are **high**, it's more **expensive** to borrow money.

- When interest rates are **low**, it's **cheaper** to borrow money.

What is compound interest?

Compound interest is interest on interest.

Compound interest calculation:

I invested $10,000 at 5% annual interest.
-On the first year my interest was
$10,000x5% =$500 interest .
At the end of the first year I had $10,500.
-On the second year the same interest is
being calculated with the new base
amount of $10,500x5%=$525
At the end of the second year I have
$11,025.
-On the third year I calculate with even
higher starting amount of
$11,025+5%=$11,576.26
and so on...

The amount we calculate the
interest from is higher every year. **That's
how we can grow our wealth.**

Credit score:

-A credit score is a number that reflects on your ability to pay back.

-It is important to keep track of your credit score.

-There are apps and websites that allows you to check your credit score and be on top of it.

-Check it regularly and try to maintain a good credit score. That way, you could borrow for less.

―――――――――

If your credit score is not good, don't worry there are ways to improve it.

You should start doing it today and not wait for tomorrow.

Having a credit card is very useful for your credit score.

Lenders and landlords check your credit score as they want to find out if you are reliable and pay your bills on time.

Keeping a credit card is a great way to spend and show that you are good at paying back.

Try to use up to 25-30% of your credit allowance, and don't apply for too many credit cards in a short time.

If you still don't have a credit card, consider one today.

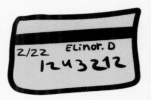

If you are forgetful and a bit overwhelmed with administration.

I suggest automatic payment to pay your bills.

This way you will never miss a payment and make sure your credit score remains high.

Chapter 8

Before we say goodbye

A few tips for you before we say
goodbye.

Don't save on insurance.
A good insurance policy will
save you money in
case you need it in the future (we all
hope we won't have to use it).
It can give you a peace of mind.
You should see it as an investment.

'**Guaranteed returns**'

Yes or no?

Nothing in life is
guaranteed apart from...
you know what (and taxes)

You should enjoy your life but always
bear in mind that
**Spending money is easy.
Earning and saving money is hard**.

Don't be fooled into thinking that
buying that special handbag or pricey
jewellery is an investment.
It is purely for pleasure.

Money will not make you happy, but not having money can make you unhappy.

We all want to be able to afford
to live the best life we can.

We want to travel, shop, have a
beautiful home, and eat in nice
restaurants.

We also want to have some money
for a rainy day, pay for education,
maybe have some money for a future
event or a big trip.

**Everyone has different dreams
But we all want to be free and have
enough money to make our dreams
come true.**

Don't put all your eggs
in the same basket.
Diversifying is the key!
Diversify your investments.
This can balance your losses
and lower your risks.

———————————

As a general rule:
The harder you want your
money to work, the more
risks you need to take.
If you don't like taking risks
you can chose a more
moderate path like bonds or
less risky shares.

If you are self-employed, use a tax consultant to advise you how to minimise your tax bill. Knowledge of **paying your taxes wisely can save you a lot of money.**

Be clever with your money!

———————————

The longer you can invest and tie up your money for, the more money you should be able to earn.
You should try to make investments for the long term. **Investments should be for at least five years upwards.**

"Where there's a tip, there's a tap".

It means where there is a
stock tip there is a "tap"
(someone who hopes to make
money off that tip).

———————————

Sophisticated investors look
for new products, new trends
and new companies and try to
spot early signs of potential
stocks.

You can do it!
- Don't be afraid of making mistakes.
- Everyone can make mistakes.
- Nobody has all the answers no matter how experienced they are.
- Trust yourself.
- You will learn with time and you will get better.

THE END

This Book is dedicated to my husband and our four kids. My family taught me you are never too young or too old to follow your dreams.

I would like to thank my son Barak who illustrated this book. Barak was always professional with endless patience and kindness.

I would like to thank **Tony Levene**. When I started investing I read his brilliant book '**Investing for Dummies**' which I highly recommend. When the idea of my book came up I contacted Tony. Tony has agreed to meet and listen to my idea, he also helped me when I wrote this book. I will always cherish his help, patience and our interesting talks over coffee.

Printed in Great Britain
by Amazon

82392477R20042